A SPECIAL SIBLING

LIFE LESSONS

FROM MY BROTHER WITH DOWN SYNDROME

JANE FEIGHERY

In loving memory
of our uncle John O'Gorman
who devoted his life to improving
the lives of those with intellectual
disabilities in Ireland, Bulgaria, and
beyond, and who loved and
delighted in his special
nephew John.

Published in October 2021
by Jane Feighery,

First edition

ISBN: 978-1-7398439-0-8

Design
by Garrett Bennis

DEDICATIONS

Dedicated to my beautiful brother John, and to my parents.

Thank you, John, for always being such a bright light in my life, and in all of our lives. Happy 30th Birthday!!!

Thank you, Mum and Dad, for the infinite dedication, patience, and ambition you have shown as John's parents. John is the wise, funny, well-adjusted person that he is thanks to his nature, but in large part thanks to the nurturing he has received also!

In particular I would like to thank my aunt and uncles who have supported, encouraged, and guided me.

A special thank you to Mary Feighery O'Gorman, Fr. John Feighery, and Conleth Feighery for the brainstorming sessions, proof-reading, and expert advice respectively.

TABLE OF CONTENTS

PREFACE

On the 10th of March 1991, my Mum received what John later described as the "best Mother's Day present", and my Dad the 'best ever birthday present'.

John Ciaran Feighery arrived at 6am; a healthy, screaming, pudgy little baby boy weighing 8 and a half pounds. It would not have been the norm back then for amnio-synthesis to be performed, nor was it something my Mum would have undertaken.

John's arrival therefore was a surprise.

As a four-and-a-half-year-old I don't remember there being any shock or grief in the air in those first few months and years of John's life during which my parents would have been adjusting to his arrival.

As a child I guess you don't know what constitutes normal or abnormal. You haven't yet learned to judge, pity or fear difference.

John, not surprisingly, was the most adorable, squidgy, and happy little baby and toddler, a precious little bundle of love, and a welcome addition to all of our lives. My Mum, a midwife by profession, adapted to and embraced the journey quite naturally, even dealing graciously and generously with a sympathy card received from a particularly concerned well-wisher. She had the support of an excellent midwife before, during and after her home birth, that of my father of course and various family members.

Her main critique of the situation in John's early years related to the lack of support offered to her as a mother. While John's physical, and psychological health were assessed with regularity, hers as the person upon whom he and all of us were dependent, was not a priority.

Nothing is particularly novel about this state of affairs given how we have historically treated mothers in Ireland, but I truly hope that the level of attention received by new mothers of babies with Special needs has drastically improved since then.

My sister Lucy was born 18 months later in 1992. Together John and Lucy became 'the little ones', two peas in a pod, the perfect play-mates, overlapping developmentally for a short period before John was overtaken and fell behind.

It was at this stage, when John was around 3, that I first started asking questions, likely because John's busy schedule of appointments was impacting on my own life as we were all dragged along in tow to each appointment in St. Vincent's on the Navan Road.

I asked my Mum why John had to go to weekly physio appointments when Lucy didn't. I had assumed that physio and speech therapy were simply activities that a baby had to engage in to learn to walk and talk, but if this were the case then it didn't compute that Lucy wasn't attending, while John still was.

I learned that John had something called Down Syndrome, and that this was why he needed to go to physio.

I took it on board, and accepted the information neutrally. When a message is delivered as clean, unbiased information we do not absorb shameful connotations with it.

Down Syndrome was not introduced to me as a loaded term, or as a negative or stigma-laden one.

It was introduced to me as a neutral, practical state of affairs. Just as John was a boy and Lucy a girl, John had something called Down Syndrome, and Lucy didn't.

Fair enough.

I did on occasion absorb feelings of discomfort, stress and tension when we were out and about with John. Specifically, I remember feeling terrified sitting in waiting rooms during visits to the old Daughters of Charity institution for people with intellectual disabilities on the Navan Road.

One occasion in particular remained imprinted in my memory; that of a visit for one of John's assessments when he was still quite little, barely a toddler I imagine.

We were sitting in a high-ceilinged waiting room in the old building surrounded by children of varying levels of ability or disability, physical and intellectual. Some were in wheelchairs. Some were screaming. Others were making other types of noises.

The place stank of institution; disinfectant so strong that the smell of it stayed on you for hours after you'd left the building. There were toys, but somehow you didn't want to risk touching them.

Overcome with fear, or absorbing the energy of the place and the situation, I began to bawl. I was about 6; old enough to feel wholly embarrassed for acting like such a baby and for making such a holy show of myself and my mother, but I was too overcome and desperate to leave to care.

I sobbed and wailed, and desperately begged my mother to take us home.

My mum curtly told me that I could go home with one of the other mother and child pairings awaiting assessment as their appointment would be over sooner than ours.

I shut my mouth and swallowed my sobs. There was no way in hell I was going home with the little boy in the wheelchair.

Little John of course was blissfully unaware of the fear, the energy, the drama, or maybe he was too young to have a memory of such events.

While my experience of institutions like this was minimal and mild, it impacted me in such a way that I physically feel waves of grief, shame, fear, and entrapment when I enter, or even hear stories about such places.

This must be an experience shared by many people born into an Ireland in which institutions were plentiful. Many of us will have had a similar experience at some point, visiting a family member or friend in a place that fits this description, and left perhaps with the same sick feeling.

Certainly, given Ireland's long love affair with institutions there must be few of us who have not stepped foot in one at some stage or another.

The purpose of this book is not to begin to unpack the effects, legacy and trauma caused by institutions for people with intellectual disabilities in our not-too-distant past, and indeed in our present day.

This is far too large and heavy a topic for me.

However, as you read the stories about the beautiful, wise, and open-hearted being that my brother is, I would like you to remember that adults, and indeed children like him, arguably THE most vulnerable and angelic members of our community, were as a rite of passage for many years put away in such grim, soulless, and clinical places, and expected to accept them as their life-long homes.

This was common practice because it was deemed that placing such people in a setting such as I have described was offering them appropriate care.

As is said, 'we did the best we could until we knew better'. This is true, and we are now doing much better. Disability services have slowly but surely improved. So much so in fact that John now receives cooking lessons via Zoom from his Daughters of Charity disability service, in which he participates from the comfort of his own kitchen, with loyal servants (my parents) on hand, should there be errors in the recipe, or missing ingredients.

INTRODUCTION

"If you have life, you have purpose."

Caroline Myss

Our ancient Irish ancestors understood the inherent value of all members of society, regardless of a person's social standing, title, abilities or talents. Indeed, they appreciated and respected not only human life, but that of all plants, animals, insects, rocks, trees, rivers, and lakes.

All of life was sacred, and our spirituality was based on this shared understanding.

Since those times, for various reasons, we have evolved to become a significantly more individualistic society; a hierarchical society that values the life of some more than that of others; that worships those things which are man-made more than the life-giving Earth; and that believes human beings to be superior to all other life on Earth, despite the atrocities we consistently commit against our fellow creatures.

Meanwhile, as per Caroline Myss' words, "if one has life, one has purpose". It is the natural order of things for it to be so. This rings true for every life-form in our eco-system, from the tiniest ant to the most sophisticated, intelligent human being.

We are each birthed onto this planet with a purpose to fulfil.

I write this book first and foremost to celebrate the first 30 years of life of my beautiful brother John, whose life, love, and way of being have so deeply impacted mine, and who pre-Covid times had for several years been planning epic celebrations for this special milestone, which will unfortunately now need to be postponed until such point at which we can again safely gather.

I write to share the unique perspectives and life lessons I have acquired thanks to the existence of this wise and happy soul.

I write because I believe it is of crucial importance at this moment in history, as we dismantle old ways and build the new, that we consciously create communities, societies and ways of living that are more compassionate, loving, caring, equal, and diverse; communities in which people like John are not just included and empowered to thrive, but also genuinely appreciated as the powerful change-makers, wisdom-holders, and leaders that they are thanks to their difference.

This is not a book about disability. It is a book about ability and innate wisdom. We typically view the terms "ability" and "disability" through such a narrow lens. We categorise people in terms of intellect while intellect is only one small part of what it means to be human, and to be alive; one small part of what is needed to follow one's purpose to lead a life worth living and leave a legacy to feel proud of.

The perception that the neuro-typical majority to which many of us belong is in any way superior to those who are neuro-diverse is unwise. We cannot categorise in such a simplistic manner.

If I moved to live in a community in which there were ten people with Down Syndrome and me living side by side, would it mean therefore that there was something wrong or lacking with my way of being and doing? Of course it wouldn't. I would be in the minority, but this shouldn't imply that I was somehow defective.

Being in the neuro-typical majority does not make one superior in any way to a neuro-diverse minority.

It is time to reframe the age-old narrative around disability, and to begin to explore the infinite abilities of the neuro-diverse with genuine curiosity and interest, asking them and ourselves what we might learn from all of these different ways of being and doing.

My intention for this book is that it be one small step along this path of curiosity, as I share with you a selection of the of the innumerable lessons I have learned from John during his first 30 years of life.

Before we begin, I would like to note that I am not an expert in the area of disability. I am the older sister of a very inspiring young man with Down Syndrome from whom I have learned a great deal.

What I express in this book is not an expert view, nor do I wish to advocate for my view being the truth.

This perspective is my truth. It is my lived experience, and these are my opinions and reflections as they relate to John.

I have consulted with John in writing this book, and have his full permission to do so. I will be reading it to him, should he wish to spare the time in his busy life to listen to me do so.

Having so often read articles or books, and watched videos relating to people with Down Syndrome which are by nature of the messaging used excluding people with Down Syndrome from their target audience, I take care in my writing about this topic to be entirely inclusive and respectful towards anyone who may choose to read this book, people with Down Syndrome (of course!) included.

My hope is that these musings will inspire others to become curious about the beauty that exists in people of all abilities, and to share their stories too.

CHAPTER 1

Lessons in Self Love

"In a society that profits from your self-doubt, loving yourself is a rebellious act."

Unknown

It is undoubtedly a radical act to love and accept oneself truly and deeply, exactly as one is. We receive an onslaught of messages from our culture persuading us that we must change ourselves in order to be enough, to be lovable, to become enlightened, or to achieve success in life.

And yet, what we are chasing in all of those achievements - the body transformations, wealth acquisitions and titles- usually comes back to our quest for love.

We believe that if we had the perfect body, partner, job, house, family, life, that we would then reach happiness rather than the other way around.

It is an undeniable if uncomfortable fact that most people pity those who have intellectual disabilities. I have heard the term 'poor fella' mentioned more times than I care to count in reference to John. The use of this phrase is automatic. It seems to be drummed deep into the consciousness of many people to consider it a 'poor' or pitiful thing to have a disability.

The irony therein which I rarely fail to note is that John is far from a 'poor' or pitiful fella. He is most likely much more content, much more fulfilled, and the giver and receiver of significantly more love than the majority.

At its core, I believe that much of John's contentment with and appreciation of his life is thanks to the simple fact that he loves himself.

We find it difficult, particularly in Ireland, to say such a phrase without grimacing, laughing or rolling our eyes. 'He loves himself' or 'she loves herself' is rarely said as a compliment. Rather it is used as a jeer, a criticism or a mockery of someone who is playing too big; someone who has stepped above their station, and is owning who they are and what they have to offer fully and unapologetically.

For most of us the journey to loving ourselves is a long and arduous one. There is so much unlearning to do. There is so much rejection of what we have absorbed from an early age about who we need to be, how we need to look, and how our life needs to evolve in order to find ourselves deserving of our own love. It is a pretty tragic state of affairs if we reflect on it for a moment. It is also a never-ending goose chase. It can only ever cause suffering to chase perfection in all aspects of one's life as a being who is by nature imperfect.

Were we born like this? Were we born feeling "less than", ignorant, problematic in our difference, or did we begin to learn it as we observed the way people are categorised, rated, and attributed different levels of worth in accordance with external achievements or aesthetics?

So many of the attributes I observe in John, some of which I will reference in this book, are born out of his deep love for himself. Without a strong sense of self-love and self-regard it is very difficult for us to develop other positive ways of being in the world that support our well-being and ability to thrive. To name a few examples, it is difficult without self-love to create and impose boundaries, to feel a sense of belonging to a community, to practice forgiveness and compassion, to speak one's truth, or to be willing to be wrong, change one's mind, or apologise with true graciousness.

I particularly note John's love and care for himself in the way he prepares for and shows up to celebrations big and small. He puts time and thought into his outfit, his hairstyle, the scent he will wear, and the combination of these three aspects. John takes great pride in wearing some form of suit, or jacket and trouser combo with a bow-tie or tie, as per the occasion, the look he is going for, and what he feels like on the day.

He is on many occasions welcomed on his arrival downstairs by an exclamation along the lines of: "Oh my God John, WHAT are you wearing?", or a similarly teasing comment, which for John is inevitably like water off a duck's back.

He will take insightful and strategic feedback from me as he considers me to be "a good picker", but any comments designed to provoke or diminish are brushed off or counteracted with a response along the lines of "Yes, I know I am so smart/stylish/handsome".

He loves being smart, stylish, and handsome, and he owns it, no holes barred.

Which is the greater winner: the person who goes back upstairs to dress themselves down, feeling silly and embarrassed for having over-dressed, or the person who holds his head high and says "Thank you, I know I am." with upmost confidence when someone genuinely, automatically, or sarcastically, comments: "You look SO smart!"?

It is surely John's unwavering self-love that keeps him true to his own unique dapper and dashing sense of style.

CHAPTER 2

Lessons in Celebrating the Little Things in Life

"The more you praise and celebrate your life, the more there is in life to celebrate."

Oprah Winfrey

We do know- that is we have been told, we have read, and yet we too regularly forget - the immense importance of appreciating and celebrating the little things in life.

Someone like John will consistently remind you of them, as he goes through his days celebrating each little thing, particularly meals, with abundant delight.

Whether its an exclamation of "I love my life" when presented with a plate of steak, potatoes and peas, or an "Oh my gosh Jane, I love you SO much" when gifted a packet of €1 Jellies, John sure knows how to genuinely savour and give thanks for every little blessing that shows up in his life.

For those of you who believe that giving thanks for that which you wish to attract in abundance will indeed result in further gifts coming your way, you can rest assured that this approach works reliably for John.

When someone shows such heartfelt appreciation for little gifts, the bestower of these gifts receives so much more than she gave in the immense gratitude she receives in return. She finds it impossible to fail to re-gift the simple gesture so easily acquired and so gleefully received.

John not only tells me with upmost sincerity that he loves me on receipt of a packet of jellies, but also sends me photos of chosen jellies for a given snack as he makes his way through them, and of the empty packet, with thanks, when he has finished them. This practice serves to both give me a warm fuzzy feeling upon the arrival of each thoughtful update, and to notify me that his supply is in need of replenishing.

Who among us can truly attest to genuinely appreciating, to the extent we might, the little aspects of our days that we are in fact thoroughly blessed to enjoy?

Without delving into controversial theories around the law of attraction, who can argue with the principle that we do indeed receive more of whatever we take the time to genuinely give thanks for, starting with the little things, like a simple, hearty meal, or the tiny gestures of sisterly love?

CHAPTER 3

Lessons in Slowing Down

"Nature does not hurry,
yet everything is accomplished."

Lao Tzu

John moves at a slower pace. He approaches each task with precision, care, and deliberation, and completes these same tasks at what for a typical person in our fast-paced culture, can feel like a painfully deliberate speed.

When sharing a life with someone with Down Syndrome, one cannot help but slow one's own pace of life. John walks more slowly, eats his meals more slowly, and gets himself up and dressed in the morning at his own glacial pace.

This common characteristic of a person like John, has undoubtedly infuriated and greatly frustrated many a family member whose life is impacted by so steady a pace, and whose pleas and demands that someone "hurry (sometimes 'the f***') up!", inevitably fall on deaf ears, and have next to no influence on the speed of the situation.

John lives his life and gets stuff done in his own sweet time. He will not be rushed, and any attempt to make him move faster is an outright waste of energy and breath.

The comment "But Jane, I AM so slow!" was uttered to me in exasperation by John one summer's evening as we were walking home along a dark country road in West Cork. I was leading the group, and as darkness fell, was beginning to doubt my knowledge of the path home, remembering just how dark it gets in rural Ireland as 10pm approaches in late summer, a far cry from the brightly-lit streets of

Madrid which I had become accustomed to walking at any hour.

I urged John to please hurry up, accusing him of walking "SO SLOWLY!"

He responded as I've outlined above, and I was put swiftly back in my box, with a dose of guilt for what now felt like quite an unkind comment.

John IS so slow, and this is simply a matter of fact.

As someone spending time in whatever context with a person with Down Syndrome, you can either accept and embrace this slower pace, or you can spend redundant time trying to change it.

A wiser option perhaps might be to learn from it, and to consider the necessity, or otherwise, of the pace at which you usually move through your life.

Does it truly serve the quality of your life, your relationships, or your work for you to move through life at full throttle, always on the clock, always wishing you had more time and space to breathe?

What would happen to your quality of life if you took a leaf from John's book and approached life more slowly, carefully, and deliberately? Might you find yourself living more consciously and contentedly?

CHAPTER 4

Lessons in Boundaries

"Daring to set boundaries is about having the courage to love ourselves, even when we risk disappointing others."

Brené Brown

So much of our contentment in life, and ultimately our satisfaction with the lives we create for ourselves, is thanks to our establishment and implementation of healthy boundaries.

Our boundaries allow us to honour our values, and therefore to live a life in accordance with what matters most to us, whether that be the activities we engage in, the people we spend time with, or how we show up for and treat those around us.

John has impeccable boundaries, and he employs them with the upmost consistency.

He sometimes outsources his boundary implementation, when he knows he can effectively do so. An example of this would be whereby he says 'yes' to something he doesn't want to eat being put on his plate by a host he does not wish to offend. He will sweetly accept the kind offer of brussel sprouts, or some other food he enjoys as little, whilst discreetly and simultaneously motioning to me or some other reliable assistant to remove them swiftly from his plate.

My favourite example of John's boundaries in action is the unapologetic protection he maintains of his relaxation time. How many of us feel sufficiently comfortable and confident to simply answer – "No, sorry, I have to relax this evening.", when asked by a well-meaning friend or family member to join them in something we would rather not do? How often do we tie ourselves in unnecessary knots due to our inability to answer with a firm "no thank you" when we wish to do so?

Might we show up more authentically and respectfully for our own needs and therefore those of our loved ones if we could graciously say "no thanks, I need to relax" as firmly, unapologetically and neutrally as John does on a regular basis?

CHAPTER 5

Lessons in Loyalty

"Things are never quite as scary when you've got a best friend."

Dr. Seuss

John has a diverse group of friends, of varying abilities, quirks and temperaments.

He will welcome whomever crosses his path, be it at Mass, at his disability service, or through his various Special Olympics activities as a 'friend', as soon as they become a regular feature in his life.

Some of these 'friends' are 50+ years older than him, some are 10+ years younger than him. Many of his older friends are people he has come to know thanks to the regularity of his Mass-going over the last 30 years. He notes their presence or absence at Mass, and he prays for them in his nightly prayer session if they are unwell.

Other friends he has met via Special Olympics are more likely people his own age with whom he regularly plays sport, or participates in athlete training programmes. This cohort is less diverse in terms of age, but more so in terms of ability, sociability, and personality.

Over the years I have been intrigued by John's openness to being friends with so diverse a group of people. He doesn't discriminate or speak judgementally of difference, or place any of the people in these various aforementioned communities into a 'non-friend' category. He has more in common with some friends than others, but those regular acquaintances with whom he could barely share a word are nevertheless categorised as friends.

The patience he demonstrates in dealing with the more hyper, anxious or unrelentingly chatty individuals is nothing short of exquisite.

I have little doubt that the limits of my own patience, and that of my other family members, friends, colleagues, etc. would buckle much more rapidly under the pressure of some of the irritating or frustrating situations I have observed John in, which he has handled with upmost grace, graciousness and ease.

It can be quite exhausting to listen to someone who repeats themselves constantly, interrupts incessantly, or is always in a hyped-up state, unable to settle down and relax. For John, being around such people is like water off a duck's back. His inner calm, and the value he holds for that person as a friend leaves him unperturbed. If it wears on him, he quietly manages his emotional state and releases the tension in healthy ways during his strictly-boundaried 'relaxation' time.

He does find other, more traditional outlets to express his frustrations of course, and much of it gets taken out on my Dad. We too frequently take less care to be kind, considerate and patient with the family members we spend most time with, and John is no exception on this front.

He finds infinite reasons for eye-rolling, head-shaking, and berating when it comes to any little thing my Dad says or does which is deemed displeasing. His impatience is rarely related to my Dad's shortcomings, and almost always linked to John's own love of drama, performance, and being a goody two-shoes, know-it-all, dictator figure in the household. He knows best how things should be done and how people should behave for all to continue running in his favour around the house.

Thankfully for my Dad, he gets to be the saviour and confidant whenever anyone else in the family steps out of line and onto one of John's toes. A self-professed 'only child' since the last of his siblings moved out 7+ years ago, John has reigned supreme ever since over the household, particularly the TV room, and the fridge.

John's large community of friends, from all walks of life and areas of his, sets him up for a quality of life which is foreign to many of us in our modern age. He invests in and values all of the relationships that come into his life, and all of the people he has met over the years.

My aunt Mary once told me a story which epitomises the situation.

One day when John was still in secondary school, Mary was tasked with walking John to school. As they walked through the relatively small park en route to the school gates, John greeted almost every person they passed with a friendly "Hi, how are you?" or some similar greeting.

Feeling a sense of responsibility to educate John on the social mores of how one interacts with strangers, Mary said to him "John, you know we usually only say hello to people like that when we know them".

John responded; “Oh but Mary I DO know them. They are all my friends!”.

Having gone for several walks with John in the fields behind our parents’ house of late, I can attest that this scenario is an entirely typical one for John.

On a recent walk several of the exchanges went as follows:

“Hi Passerby, how are you?”

“Oh, Hi John, I’m good thanks, how are you? You’re looking well!”

“Thanks Passerby. I know I am.”

Each of these exchanges was followed by me asking who the person was and receiving a lowdown from John on how he knew them, and the history of the friendship.

Imagine the social support networks and sense of belonging to communities we would all have if we invested the same level of loyalty, compassion, and care in tending to our ordinary, every-day relationships as John does?

By moving through life at a slower pace there is more presence and attention available for each of the people with whom John interacts, and there is also a level of respect and non-judgement which many of us have to work to achieve.

Knowing John as I do, and seeing the way in which he engages with these friends, I have zero doubt that their lives are every bit as enriched by his friendship as his is by theirs.

CHAPTER 6

Lessons in Tenderness

"There is no charm equal to tenderness of heart."

Jane Austen

From the moment he entered our family John introduced immeasurable levels of tenderness, love and affection into a family culture similar to that of many other Irish families from the point of view of emotional expression and the attitudes towards it.

Children rapidly absorb and learn to mimic the behavioural patterns of their parents; how they walk, how they talk, how they express themselves emotionally or otherwise.

People like John, I believe thanks to a learning disability, remain much truer and closer to source than the more easily-moulded neuro-typical human child. They continue therefore to give and receive love and tenderness more vulnerably, whole-heartedly and all-encompassingly than their more self-conscious, socially-aware peers do.

As a child, John was forever the person in the family that could be relied upon to sense and respond accordingly to heightened emotional states, in the most caring and concerned of ways. If somebody was upset John would express genuine concern and engage with him or her with complete dedication, presence, and interest in their pain.

He would ask lots of questions about what was wrong; open-ended questions, or sometimes leading questions, depending on the injustices he had been on the receiving end of on a given day.

I remember him walking into my room when I was about 12, and he was 8, his eyes widening with concern and his jaw dropping when he saw that I was upset. He came over and enquired as to what was wrong. I said I was fine, but he wasn't satisfied. His expression changed to a more knowing one, and he said "Was it Mum??"

He continued: "I KNOW it was Mum that did this to you! She SO horrible today! Earlier she say to me 'NO JOHN, you CANNOT watch telly'. It's okay Jane, don't worry, she's just horrible."

If his genuine concern wasn't enough to lift your spirits, John's analysis of a situation, and its refreshingly unique and dramatic tone never fails to move you directly from tears to laughter, rapidly dispersing whatever dark cloud was present.

Far too many of us that grow up in families and societies which repress emotion lose the ability to respond to someone in pain without first putting an impenetrable, protective shield around ourselves to ensure we not absorb any of this shameful emotional incontinence and, thereby we show up ill-equipped to support a fellow human being who simply needs to be seen, heard, understood, and cared for.

John excels in embodying these aspects in his response to people's emotional outpourings. He shows up entirely open, deeply caring, and equipped with a desire to understand and remedy what is wrong. He also reliably brings levity and humour to a situation, elevating the mood rapidly, and dispersing any embarrassment or tension. He is immensely skilled in the art of emotional attunement.

Consistently showing affection to loved ones who are less affectionate themselves, he can transition with ease from playing the role of long-suffering teenager to the role of concerned motherly, fatherly, or brotherly figure towards anyone in the family when he senses a requirement to do so.

Another example of John's interest and concern for others was apparent when he was a little boy. His jaw would drop if he saw someone on crutches, in a wheelchair, or in any way physically compromised. He would turn to me, or the nearest reliable question-answerer and whisper "Oh my God, poor thing, what happened?".

It is the tenderness, love, affection, and compassion that someone like John brings into a family, a workplace, or any community he enters that I believe is possibly one of the most valuable aspects of coming into contact with so unsullied a soul.

Having had the benefit of John's existence in my life since the tender age of four and a half, I find it somewhat bizarre and also quite sad that it is so often considered that a service or favour is being done to someone like John when he is given a job, allowed to attend a mainstream school, or to be included in any activity not specifically offered for people of different abilities.

It is as if those of us in the neuro-typical majority assume that just because we are in the majority that our way of being must therefore be superior.

It is as if we forget time and time again that one's satisfaction in life comes down to the love he has given and received, not the degrees or titles he has achieved and earned.

We miss so many deeply transformative and valuable learning opportunities by failing to be as caringly, compassionately curious about John's way of being, as he is about that of other people.

Imagine having the joy of a beautifully caring, compassionate and loving being added to your family, workplace or community? How could you not want that addition!

CHAPTER 7

Lessons in Presence

"Wherever you are, be totally there."

Eckhart Tolle

One of the most popular wellness trends sweeping the world over the last decade has been that of Mindfulness. Mindfulness is defined as maintaining a moment-by-moment awareness of our thoughts, feelings, bodily sensations and surrounding environment through a gentle and nurturing lens. It teaches us how to be more present, to live in the moment rather than in the past or the future, to show up fully engaged for whomever we are with, or whichever task we are focused on.

John has attended many a Mindfulness session over Zoom during Covid times. For months he called it 'mind influence', and I selfishly regret correcting this ironic play on words as it made me laugh every time I heard it pronounced.

Eckhart Tolle asserts that one of the reasons we have so much difficulty at times in recollecting the past is due to the fact that we were not in fact present for it. We often have much more vivid and emotive recollections of the experiences we had as children, before our 'ordinary thinking mind', or beta brainwave state began to dominate.

As adults spend most of our time in a beta brainwave state, whereas young children will cycle between delta, theta, beta and alpha depending on their phase of development.

In a meditative practice much of the work we are doing is aimed at moving us out of beta, and into a state of heart-coherence, a state in which we are connecting with the much deeper wisdom of the heart and body, while slowing the activity of the overbearing monkey mind which is constantly trying to run the show.

John has an exceptionally good memory, and I have a hunch that it relates to his ability to be present, thanks potentially to his cycling between several brain states rather than spending an inordinate amount of time in beta like the majority of us. This theory of mine is based entirely on my own observation of John's way of being over the years, and is further supported by his remarkable ability to fall asleep within moments of closing his eyes for a rest.

Just how good his memory is can often be missed due to his memories not being shared, and therefore not being validated by those around him. It is also missed due to the inability of others to read his mind, and know exactly what he's hinting at when he expects that if a hint is obvious to him it should be just as obvious to anyone else who was present for a given scenario.

A long-time reader of John's mind, I can usually very quickly deduce exactly what he is referring to, when based on a given conversation, he begins a "Do you remember when..." question.

It is partly because I have forever known exactly what John loves, what information he consumes, and what will most impact him. Having a life-long interpreter at one's side must be a convenient state of affairs!

CHAPTER 8

Lessons in Healthy Optimism

"If you can't do anything about it,
don't worry about it."

Jeanne Calment

Observing the peaks and troughs of John's relationship to Covid restrictions and the lockdowns we have undergone over the last year has been nothing short of heartening.

Like so many of us John has had moments of hope that the cloud is finally lifting, and that life might soon get 'back on track' as he consistently phrases it. He has also had moments of utter frustration and disappointment when a lockdown is again extended, or another one is introduced.

What has remained constant throughout, however, is a hopeful and optimistic attitude that things will indeed soon get 'back on track', which he fuels with the excitement he feels in anticipation of again being able to go swimming, play football, go to the Blanchardstown Shopping Centre, see his friends at his service, and attend Respite, etc.

He notes the planned re-opening dates for certain facilities or services, and then excitedly looks forward to these dates with a level of glee and delight that most people are failing to muster at this stage. When a given reopening date is pushed back or renegotiated, John doesn't fall in a heap under a burst bubble of excitement, he simply replaces the previous date with the updated one, and says "Oh my God I can't wait for 'insert new date' to arrive!".

This is buoyancy at its best. It's an in-built resilience mechanism of non-attachment that so many spiritual seekers spend years or lifetimes working to embed. It's an ability, or a choice arguably, to feel all of the joy, gratitude and excitement for an event before it has happened, thereby fuelling one's every-day existence with these feelings, and the chemicals – namely, dopamine and serotonin – that accompany them, while being able to bounce straight back when the event is cancelled or postponed.

John will not lend an ear to the doubters or the realists in his midst; those concerned mostly about protecting him from the future disappointment he may feel.

I have on occasion been the realist, responding to his excitement with a doubtful "Hmmm", or a comment beginning with "John, I'm not so sure..." which is reliably interrupted and cut short, because he doesn't care to hear what I was going to say.

On Easter Monday 2020 John told me in an upbeat tone that Leo[1] had said that the virus would be gone by May, and so life would be back on track by then. My response was sceptical, and was promptly dismissed. If Leo said one thing and Jane said another, it was obvious as to which view held greater weight as far as John was concerned.

If we can use our faith and hope that all will indeed work out as fuel to keep us contentedly ticking along while we weather the storm of lockdowns, then why not do so? It is an immune-booster to feel so much gratitude, excitement, and hope. It allows for a much more pleasant lockdown experience as the feelings and chemicals associated with future freer times are already being stimulated

[1]*Leo Varadkar is an Irish Fine Gael politician who served as Taoiseach (Prime Minister) from 2017 to 2020.*

in the body, and the associated thoughts are already circulating in the mind. John is unwittingly living in line with the findings of modern neuroscience, and the ancient teachings of the Yoga tradition along with many other wisdom teachings. He does so not because he has been taught to do so, or thanks to having studied neuroscience or yoga philosophy. He does so because he naturally ignores and is protected from much of what circulates in the world, and because he chooses to think, feel and act on what makes him feel good.

Could it really be that simple?

Might it be that understanding and complying with current restrictions, noting when they will end, and then disconnecting from the daily/hourly/minute-by-minute news bulletins might in fact be really positive for our state-of-mind?

John only cares about the information that will serve him to create events to look forward to, and to know what he is allowed to do right now. Otherwise, he shields himself from copious amounts of negative news which has no doubt served his health royally.

CHAPTER 9

Lessons in Apologising

"A great man is always willing to be little."

Ralph Waldo Emerson

Apologising is a skill which a minority of people truly master, or appreciate enough to do so. The strength and clinging of one's ego and therefore one's attachment to being right can be relentless, and too many people go through life thinking that their apologising for wrongs they have committed will set them back rather than lighten their load.

Many people consistently 'apologise' in a way that immediately undermines the apology. For example, by saying; "I'm sorry you were hurt by what I said", rather than "I'm sorry for hurting you". In the first iteration, instead of taking responsibility for the hurt incurred, it is implied by the person apologising that the responsibility for feeling hurt lies with the recipient of the hurtful comment rather than with the person who made it.

Often, when those close to us call us out on being unkind, out-of-line, or rude, we enter into an intellectual battle, investing in justifying our righteousness, and then standing firmly and unwaveringly in it, possibly adding insult to injury and allowing the argument to fester, or to blow up further.

John, like to many of his contemporaries, lives from his heart more so than from his head, which is an infinitely refreshing, sensible, and grounded way to live.

He has an ego of course, as we all do, and he does not like being wrong, corrected, or told he was out of line.

The difference however, which I have noted over the years relates again to resilience, choice of attitude, and quite simply, to humility.

It depends on the situation of course, and there are a few ways it can play out. Sometimes a door has been slammed and someone has stomped up the stairs before there has been an opportunity to explain why and how something was out-of-line. In this case a conversation ten minutes later can resolve the issue.

Whether the resolution happens in the moment or shortly thereafter, it usually plays out in such a way that John receives the criticism with a frown, a general look of cynicism and a cool if not frigidly cold demeanour. He may respond with a gruff, dismissive, one-worded answer such as "okay", or "right", and then leave the room or make it clear that the person addressing him should leave his. Filthy looks, a scowl, and loud sighs are all part of the course.

Then (and this is what blows me away every single time!), John will seek the complainant out within a space of time as short as ten to twenty minutes, arriving with a sunny demeanour, a fresh perspective, a genuine apology, an acknowledgment that he now understands what he shouldn't have done and why, and a promise to never do it again. Sometimes this promise is accompanied by a showering of gratitude, offerings or additional promises. Sometimes the promises are highly aspirational.

"I will never eat sweets again!" would be one such aspirational promise.

Nevertheless, I consistently find such exchanges exceptionally humbling relative to similar exchanges with other family members or loved ones over the years.

How is it that someone with a learning disability finds it so much easier to understand the reasoning behind something being unfair or inappropriate while a neuro-typical person cannot?

Therefore I have a couple of suggestions.

John, and maybe others like him, is open to understanding and learning what he may have done wrong. His mind has not battened down the hatches or convinced him to close his ears. He is genuinely listening, and he is doing so with an open mind as well as a particularly open heart.

Furthermore, when we live from the heart and listen with our hearts, we are less self-righteous and therefore more inclined to produce genuine, heartfelt apologies, free from additional intellectualisation or posturing to subtly reinstate our opinion or view, which of course reliably results in further back-and-forth, and potentially an additional argument to work through.

CHAPTER 10

Lessons in Vulnerability

"Staying vulnerable is a risk we have to take if we want to experience connection."

Brené Brown

Many people feel somewhat socially awkward in the presence of someone like John. Aside from what are hopefully now outdated views that a learning disability might bring shame or stigma on those associated with it, I believe that much of what causes people to feel unsure of themselves in the presence of John is their usual reliance on social mores. Usually, we are surrounded by people with whom we share unwritten codes of behaviour.

One is secretly, and possibly even unconsciously, afraid that someone like John will say or do something outside the confines of these unwritten rules, and that this, or indeed their inability to respond in a manner they can rely on, will make them look silly, weak or vulnerable.

It could be loosely compared perhaps to arriving to a foreign country in which one doesn't speak the language, or understand the cultural norms, and accidentally becoming a laughing stock or deeply offending someone due to one's own ignorance.

For the people unused to seeing someone like John as 'one of us' who suddenly find themselves needing to interact with him, the awkwardness is akin to a significantly amplified version of the 'making a fool of oneself in a foreign country' scenario described above. Many people freeze or become really quite awkward. They may speak very loudly or as if they were speaking to a child, or they may even ignore his presence altogether; a response I have observed quite regularly.

It is quite common for people to not understand what is being communicated by someone like John, and when this happens, they usually become visibly anxious rather than simply asking for further detail on what it was they didn't understand, and continuing to enquire until it lands with them.

I have never not understood what John was trying to say, because if ever I don't catch a certain word, I will enquire in a variety of ways until the point has landed. Such interactions when undertaken from a place of mutual respect and zero-judgement or embarrassment are mutually rewarding and relationship-deepening. They leave both parties feeling content and understood, and therefore the relationship can be trusted and settled into.

For those who feel anxious about such an interaction, I would advise asking for whatever it was you did not understand to be phrased in a different way. You can ask for a description of the word you don't understand, or for it to be spelled out for you. It may of course be spelled incorrectly, but that doesn't matter, because it gives a further clue. Ask these questions in an interested and respectful manner until you arrive at the point, or get to the heart of the matter at hand.

Part of the fear of course in dealing with someone whose idea of social appropriateness may not fit with yours is that this person may say or do something you deem entirely inappropriate.

Let me reassure you that this most likely will

occur on occasion, or even on a regular basis, depending on the character involved, and that it will often involve a comment more truthful than others would dare to utter, which is usually hilarious, and often hits the nail firmly on the head.

I consider it a privilege and a contributor of great richness to my life to regularly be on the receiving end of, or in the midst of, such truth bombs.

I am reminded to not take myself, or life, too seriously, and how my presence is experienced is reflected back to me significantly more authentically than it is from others who are ensuring to be polite.

A little truth bomb story for you.

On Christmas Day 2019 we had a large group visiting my family home including lots of aunts, uncles and cousins from far and wide. My Mum was intensely busy in the kitchen, and my brother Luke asked how he could help. She requested he encourage people to start taking their seats at the table, and Luke responded by delegating the task directly to John, as he does, to make sure John is being useful. John agreed to do so and then strolled over to the nearest group of people, joined their conversation, and failed to ask anyone to sit down.

A few minutes later I asked my Mum what I could do to help and she made the same request. I promptly raised my voice, interrupted everyone, and asked them to take a seat at the table.

Luke glared at John, shaking his head and saying; "John, I told YOU to do that 5 minutes ago!".

John coolly looked directly at me while responding to Luke and pronounced, "Well I guess I'm just not harsh enough."

Such brutally and beautifully truthful comments from John are commonplace.

Personally, I adore them! They keep me in line.

CHAPTER 11

Lessons from a Creature of Habit

"We are what we repeatedly do.
Excellence then is not an act, but a habit."

Aristotle

Stubbornness is a temperament often quoted as a characteristic of Down Syndrome. While I have witnessed John, and friends of his, behaving in ways which appear stubborn, it is a descriptor which I feel is often unfairly narrow, and can reflect a biased view used to describe a whole myriad of potential situations through one fixed lens.

What I have often observed, which I believe can be mistaken for stubbornness at times, is a preference to stick to one's own routine and way of doing things, rather than bend without complaint and go compliantly along with the preferred way of doing things, or the plans perhaps of another person who is deemed the decision-maker because he or she is the neurotypical one, the parent, or the caregiver.

All human beings thrive with routine, with an estimated 95% of our daily thoughts being the same as those of the previous day, repeated automatically thanks to our subconscious programming rather than created by our executive brain. Therefore, day after day we are most likely, unless we apply significant conscious effort to do otherwise, to repeat the same routines, behaviours and thought-patterns of days gone by. This can serve us when we have positive and healthy habits, over time supporting us to thrive. It can also be hugely detrimental when we have unhealthy habits.

As is the case for everyone, John's day-to-day is made up of and determined by the habits he has learned and embedded over the years.

Like you and me, he has some habits that are healthier than others. He drinks copious amounts of water, forever bemused and disapproving of how little I drink. He also has less healthy habits such as his 11pm pre-bedtime snack, which reliably contains both sugar and carbs but has at least latterly been reduced in size.

It is true that John is unimpressed and not inclined to want to comply if someone comes along and tries to interfere with his routine. If I were to arrive home and say; "Scrap everything you had planned, you're coming out with me for the evening.", John would politely but firmly decline my offer, unless he really would prefer to do what I was proposing instead of what he had planned.

Imagine being someone whose needs, preferences, or desires are often misunderstood, misinterpreted, or simply dismissed.

Imagine how it would feel to be treated like the 8-year-old child that has to slot into his parents' plans when you're 20-something years old?

Might it be entirely justified to reject new plans which are neither yours, nor to your liking, and insist on sticking to your own?

Absolutely! It is 100% justified.

I have the upmost respect for John's firm rejection of plans he does not want to be a part of, and I respect also the desire and need to rigorously control one's schedule that someone so at the behest of others' schedules must feel.

If John declines an offer to do something that I genuinely feel would benefit and enrich him, I sow a few discreet seeds of motivation, scarcity, and excitement, and then leave him to make the choice himself when he's reflected on it. So often in these situations he does decide to join in on whatever it is, be it jigsaw-making, cake-baking, or going for a walk. It may happen that the cake is conveniently already baked by the time he has decided to take joint responsibility and credit for it, but he has improved greatly on this front thanks to his openness to new experiences during Covid times.

John has transpired to be a model of the benefits of being a stubborn creature of habit since we entered into our first lockdown in March 2020.

In the absence of his usual daily Special Olympics activities, he began going for (long) daily walks by himself, usually clocking between 10,000 and 15,000 steps per day.

These daily walks were not embraced at first. They came about after a week or so of regular negotiations between my parents and John on the topic, with John becoming irritated by the random and regular reminders that he must interrupt his day and go for a walk.

After a week or so of irritation and frustration, he took ownership of the matter, parked the arguments, and simply agreed to go for two walks per day, on his own terms and schedule, and has been doing so ever since.

Thanks to his stubbornness and love of routine, John is significantly healthier, lighter, and fitter than he was pre-Covid.

If you have someone like John in your life therefore, my advice would be to invest consistently early on in motivating and inspiring them to develop healthy habits, and to be respectful also of their own agency and right to choose whether or not to do things your way, or to go along with your plans.

It is so important in our dealings with someone like John that we always check the inherent power imbalance which exists by virtue of the respective communication abilities, and be generous of time, spirit and willingness to understand his point-of-view and reasoning before insisting on the validity of our own.

CONCLUSION

These lessons I have learned from John are far from original as per the age-old and new-age wisdom plentifully available in the Self-Help section of any bookshop.

What I believe to be original however is the idea that a person with a learning disability so effortlessly and naturally embodies ways of being which for some of us take a lifetime (or several) to learn, and that many of us will sadly never learn.

As my mother commented recently "it's easy for him", because he doesn't have the same responsibilities, worries and challenges as most people do. While I agree that he doesn't have the same challenges as someone responsible for making their own way in life, I also have no doubt that the challenges associated with constantly feeling different, dependent, and misunderstood must be pretty exhausting at times.

In light of these challenges, I consider it even more admirable that his positivity levels remain so consistently high. For some of John's peers positivity levels are not always so well-balanced, and oftentimes it is due to a keen awareness that they do not fit in, and that they are less valued and cherished in society than they deserve to be. Any awkward situations in which you are seen to be the odd one out are undoubtedly significantly more devastating for the person who is believed to be odd than they are for the other person or people.

Regardless, John has taught me that being a

content, happy and successful person is not a complex feat. Indeed it is by over-complicating it that we succeed in making ourselves unhappy.

Gratitude and appreciation for all of the little things in life is our starting point, along with a deep love and respect for ourselves. For many of us there is much unlearning to do before we can arrive at John's levels of self-love and gratitude for what is. We have taken on infinite layers of conditioning which tell us that there are certain things we need to achieve, or milestones we need to reach before we can allow ourselves to love and accept ourselves. Could you imagine simply dropping all of the "shoulds" and loving yourself exactly as you are? What a relief that could be.

There is so much to be gained for all of us in welcoming and genuinely valuing diversity in our schools, sports-grounds, workplaces, and communities, and my main objective in writing this book has been to illustrate that. Having someone like John in your life is a gift.

It is a crying shame for us to miss out on the beautiful wisdom that emanates from people of different abilities, as so many of the lessons they teach us are exactly those we need to learn in order to evolve into a more compassionate, loving, inclusive and joyful society.

On a more serious note, we will discover, should we choose to educate ourselves on it, that we are living in a world which can be heartless in its rejection of beings who do not tick certain boxes, and increasingly "ambitious" with regard to the feats of science and how it can control the future reproductive fate of our species.

Arguably we have for a long time lived in a world which treated such people as second-class citizens, with previous generations excluding them in exceptionally cruel ways, namely through institutionalisation.

The difference in our modern world is by virtue of the scientific discoveries that have been made, and the technologies created to support them.

Covid too has had a devastating effect on the lives of many people with learning disabilities, particularly for those who contracted it and for whom the dangers have usually been higher, and the ability to fight for the right to ventilators, and life-saving interventions lower.

Each person's journey through life is his or her own to navigate, and I am fully respectful of the difficult choices people must sometimes make, along with the much harsher and heavier side of this story which involves the reality of becoming a life-long carer for someone who will never be independent, as is most often the case.

The invitation I leave you with, very simply, is that starting as and where you are, you begin to reflect with curiosity, with a genuine sense of equality, and with love towards those you come across who are not neuro-typical; that any sense of there being something 'wrong' with them dissolves from your perception of reality, and that you consider that interactions and relationships with such people may indeed benefit you even more than it benefits them.

John Feighery is a busy man, now 30 years of age. John is the third of four children to parents Ruth and Ciaran. He attended St. Mochta's National School, Clonsilla and Castleknock Community College. His parents worked tirelessly to ensure his needs were catered for in mainstream education, and he was blessed with excellent Special Needs Assistants (SNAs) in both schools. Since leaving school he has been attending the disability day services provided by his local service provider, the Daughters of Charity.

He is an active sportsman, participating weekly in many Special Olympics activities with Sports Club 15, including soccer, basketball, floorball, swimming, and dancing, among others.

John loves a good Mass, and enjoys the sociability of being involved in his local parish just as much. He has been serving Holy Communion at Mass for many years, and also serves tea, orange juice and biscuits afterwards. He has performed in the annual parish pantomime for 10+ years, and somehow wins the 'Best Actor' award every year.

Having begun his career in Starbucks while still in secondary school, John has gone on to work in a variety of settings, most recently in a trendy gastropub in Blanchardstown Village. He greatly missed these jobs when Covid struck, and busied himself instead with daily walks, Zoom dance classes, cooking classes, karaoke, mindfulness sessions, and many hours on YouTube.

John's favourite hobbies include relaxing, watching Eastenders, Father Ted, and Friends, and spending time with his girlfriend Aisling, his best friend Jack, and his many other friends from his disability service and Special Olympics.

Jane Feighery is an Executive Coach, Business Consultant and Yoga Teacher based in Dublin, with 10+ years' experience in a variety of sectors ranging from US Tech to social enterprise to the wellness industry.

A graduate of Smurfit Executive Business School's Diploma in Corporate Governance, Jane also holds a BA in Modern Languages and a Post-graduate Diploma in International Business Development from The University of Manchester and DIT respectively. She is a certified Story Coach, and holds an Advanced Practitioner Diploma in Coaching with Neuroscience.

Thanks to having John as her younger brother, Jane takes a keen interest in the value to society of those of different abilities, and shares snippets of John's wisdom wherever she goes.

Printed in Great Britain
by Amazon

75276902R00052